SONGS OF SANGFROID

THIS IS YOUR POETRY BOOK.

DIYA MALHOTRA

To those who helped me piece together a broken mirror. Still cracked, merely fragments glued together, it still lets me see who I am today. May this book allow me to do the same for you, to hand you fragments, hoping one fits in your mirror.

Contents

Contents

Contents

Preface

In this book, dwell the secrets I could never whisper to another's ear. In this book, lie the memories that entangle my world. In this book, I keep safe all the words I could never say until now. Now I sing these words to you. As for the memories and secrets, maybe we can share a few.

1. Songs of Sangfroid

• 1 •

It's the words you hear the most,
when your branches crack and flowers droop.
When the waves crash too loud to hear any tune.
Read, my song of sangfroid.

2. Corridor of Memories

I marched out that corridor for the last time, about a decade back.

Evocation blurred through the window, as time trickled away.

Certainly, I had moved on from them.

Yesterday, I stepped foot into that corridor again.

Very well knowing I let most souvenirs slip.

Knowing I would unearth them all over again.

To unimaginable shock, with every tap of my foot against the ashen cement,

a new memory hurled behind my eyes.

They were obscured, not blurred, I learned.

I gaurded them as closely as a bottle does to a letter delivered across sea.

So much so, that on ordinary days, even I stood in front of a keyless door.

I found, memories don't drift away.

A memory couldn't possibly be smoke from a candle or a fading train whistle.

It's cosmic clockwork, the way we revolve around them.

The theives keeping robbing, the shifting sand slips,

and the corridor becomes the foundation on which I march, everyday.

3. Hoax

Follow blindly,
walk on footprints already carved in the soil.
You'd find yourself walking in a rut,
a typical hoax.
Climb out while your limbs still hold might,
unravel your blindfold,
let your own feet guide you through the soil.

4. Somewhere between J-02 and S-02

Somewhere between J-02 and S-02, I grew up.

I never thought I would.

Sitting in the front of the Junior-02 bus, the new blue clothed seats.

I admired my seniors, who chatted away in the backseats, looking forward to the day I would too.

The buses seldom changed, from roaring two seaters to luxurious leathered three seaters.

Years passed, I ended up in the same decade-old bus with blue clothed seats, now full of dust.

It's plastic covering vandalised with memories.

Nothing changed, yet everything did.

The name changed from Junior-02 to Senior-02, but I still felt the same- a 4 year old child, who was now rising 18, somehow.

I now sat at the backseat I once admired, wishing to once again be young enough to sit at the front.

It's funny how 14 years later, I still entered my school bus with wishful eyes.

Where'd all the time go?

Somewhere between J-02 and S-02, I grew up.

I never thought I would.

5. Wait

To wait, to yearn for better is all we've ever been taught to do.

Wait.

Till there isn't enough time left to dream of another tomorrow.

"Lose and let go, it's for tomorrow".

But you said that yesterday, and today, it is still lost.

Why was I made to let go, when I could have held it from the very beginning?

6. The Juggler's Rhapsody

In a whirlwind of disorder, a juggler's attention stays
unbroken.
A symphony of hands, powerfully woven.
"Throw, catch, throw, catch, throw, catch..."
The juggler repeats the words in their head while drowning
out the roars of the audience.
Within the glaring spotlight's radiant beam,
the juggler's vision, undeterred, stays keen.
Each prop takes flight, defying gravity's pull,
as if time suspends its relentless rule.
"Throw, catch, throw, catch, throw, catch..."
A mantra that echoes in their mind,
guiding the cadence of their practiced hands.
The juggler strives to achieve balance,
to achieve perfect symphony with the props.
"Throw, catch, throw, catch, throw, catch..."
Every throw, a vulnerable moment.
Every catch, a brief glimpse of relief.
"Throw, catch, throw, catch, throw, catch..."
The rhythm pulses through the juggler's veins.
Each prop in the air given undivided attention.

The juggler strives to manage the most complicated juggling act.

• 7 •

7. Cloth

•

You tell your tale in the same tune every time.

It'd be a shame if they knew you were pulling the wool over
their eyes.

This fabrication,

what if I told them all you ever say,

is a thread you tore from your cloth of lies.

8. Your Shrine

You.
Once, twice, thrice,
and a countless times.
Take a pair of kind eyes for granted again,
and again,
and again.
Place guilt and remorse where your blind spot lies.
Do you pretend your shrine in ruins,
stands tall and golden like it did before?
Do you choose to do it all over again?
Me.
Building it back again,
from ruins scattered across lands.
Holding undying faith in unguided hope.
If told you I was restoring the fallen monument,
would you join me too?
Does the vision of it rebuilt, stronger, guide you too?

9. Train Ride

I've been on a train ride.

For two decades, give or take.

Every millisecond, my choices build the tracks this train travels on.

I catch myself worrying about these tracks.

After all, where could they lead?

My mind ran always 10 times faster than the train.

I so easily forget that it's okay to pause,

To peek through the window and steal glances with the pristine view.

It's an endless stride,

One I'm willing to take.

10. A Royal Masquerade

A royal masquerade.

Identities adorned in ornate guise.

Veiled behind clusters of pixels and pseudonyms,

the digital sovereigns.

A royal masquerade.

Where anonymity reigns supreme.

A play of deception begins.

A royal masquerade.

Every interaction, scripted.

Orchestrated, like a precisely choreographed ballet.

A royal masquerade.

The web, often, can be of lies.

A puzzle indeed, to find authenticity in artifice.

The digital world you prize is nothing,

but a royal masquerade.

11. Wave

I thought of you as a wave,

a common metaphor for those who sway back and forth.

Today, I see you as clearly as ever,

the high tide that never chose to leave.

A tide that always softly enveloped every inch of who I chose

to be.

I always thought of you to be behind me.

Not lesser, but a glimmering current to only admire.

Today, I choose to take a step back, to gleam beside you.

I see my reflection in you, grinning brighter than ever.

And I find myself,

wanting to thank every wave to ever carry me, to bring me

back to you.

12. If I Had Nine Lives

If I had nine lives,

You wouldn't be able to tell they're all mine.

One creates. The second loves.

The others protest, battle, protect.

Some learn, some teach. Some help.

I write.

But I try to live the lives of nine.

To become me, they all intertwine.

13. Canvas

Yes, life is a canvas, that you must fill and paint on your own.
Heard that a lot, haven't you?
Not today.
Today, the canvas is a theatre.
Curtains up.
Shadows and light engage in a tango, casting a chiaroscuro spell on the scene.
Hues emerge and merge as characters enter, like brushstrokes taking their cue.
With every movement, each character, like a stroke, reveals a layer of subtext and emotive resonance.
The canvas is peppered with cryptic smears, when tension heightens, locking out visitors in suspense.
Curtains down.

14. The Glue Between Your Tiles

They don't know if they're being led on or if you're oblivious.

They tell themself, "I'm turning into a tile, isn't it obvious?"

After a cloying moment of hope,

they recognise their own naivety.

Nothing new.

Once again,

they had thought that when you were taking them,

to another patch of barren land,

you were turning them into a tile.

Once again,

you misled them.

For all you were doing is holding them close.

Not like a tile,

but a bottle of glue.

To help patch on some other tile of your choosing.

Glue, again.

They seeped between your tiles,

Nothing but enmity in their eyes.

Dead on their feet, they decided to run.

They kept an eye on you,

while increasing the gap between you and them.

But you,

you fiddled while Rome burned.

Enough, they had.

They cast a blind eye.

There were days when they held their breath while walking through the air you exhaled.

But every moment of your ignorance increased the degree their blood boiled at.

Finally, beside themself with emotion only they could imagine,

they gave up on you.

Finally, they decided to build their own floor.

And unlike you,

they didn't need someone to be the glue for their own tiles.

You tiles slowly started to break apart.

You were left alone.

But them?

You left them, well beyond caring.

15. On Your Own

To be on your own,

is the bravest thing you can be.

To collect obliging beams:

constantly, yet none consistently.

To prize each as eternal,

while being cognizant of their transience.

Only such acceptance has the power to mend.

16. My Olive Branch

Here lies my olive branch,
I'll send the dove to give you a piece.
Let it mend your scars,
Allow your hurt to cease.

17. Silence

More ordinary than assumed.

However peaceful,

silence is overlooked.

Often shattered by minds, our own.

When piped down,

tranquility is known.

Silence is much like a pause,

where musings meld.

It is stillness.

The font of introspection's stream.

Life, a vacant chalice thirsting to be filled,

sometimes finds solace in hollowness.

It is quiet.

Where all expression is wordless.

Almost as if a riddle,

a riddle holding sagacity's touch.

18. Roots

Between us,
somehow,
how deep our roots ground in the soil
do not determine the lengths to which we grow.
Yesterday, I knew us to be planted on grounds miles apart.
Today, I find our stems to be entangled in a way,
only mimicked by the way our stories interlock.

19. Built from Broken Branches

I watch them stumbling,
the harsh rocks make it downhill.
With torn wings, and stained eyes.
I knead through the broken soil.
They stray in my undoing.
I gather the torn, fibrous roots.
With the dissolution of their faith, I am born.
They were buried, ripped away,
yet still worth assembly.
Freed from the weight of expectation,
my feet ground firmly.
I revolt with a glint of zeal.

20. Years

It'll take time,

I thought, 5 years ago.

There was supposed to be so much,

between then and now.

Yet I spend every new year,

training myself to write the year not as it was, two years ago.

Maybe it went by fast because things were the same.

I know this year carries greater change.

Then why, still, is the clock ticking faster every passing minute?

I realise, that I don't.

2 years ago, wasn't just yesterday.

2 years ago is someone whose words are a mere haze today.

To visualise the construct of time is to forget,

to realise the ever increasing distance between you and the person 2 years ago.

21. Nani House

'Nani house', my sanctuary, my second home.

Within its walls, my heart finds solace, and memories roam.

But bidding farewell to nani, as my car pulls away,

leaves my soul heavy, yearning for one more day.

Nani house, it reminds me of my nanu.

He raised me like no other.

He raised me to be bold.

He taught me to stay curious, to explore, to invent.

His teachings, I will forever hold.

Everytime I create something, it is only an ode to him.

22. Happy Mother's Day

As a newborn baby or an adult,
your arms have always been the safest place to be.
I only wish for you to know, how dear you are to me.
Everyday, the first thing I see is your beaming smile.
Everyday, you sacrifice so much for me,
be it time, comfort, or taking the raisins from my cereal.
We share laughter and sometimes argue,
and through it all, I love you.
Mumma, I hope to make you as happy as you make me,
every single moment of every single day.
You will always be the best part of me.

23. Romanticise

They lift their quill,
Feathers so tranquil.
Honey tinted eyes aflame,
The wilder heart, who's to tame?
The fire of dawn rabid,
Winsome freckles illuminated.

24. You Know Her

Brought unease, vision deluded.

Their nerves as good as violin strings amidst the unknown.

But she rose.

For a moment, it was all hers.

What they couldn't see, they feared.

What she couldn't see, she owned.

She flew with fearless abandon.

Until the final stroke of midnight.

Until the sky set ablaze.

She had no choice, but to nod and listen,

Until she could rise again, the silver sentinel.

25. Never Ending

The moment bounding leaps took place of my daily trudge,

was the moment I knew.

Teeming with possibility.

I'm only a cloth.

Whose every stitch is a testament to my devotion.

Only a placid lake.

Reflecting the vibrancy of the lovestruck.

Bearing no resemblance to the ones from my past, I'm certain,

it'll always be.

26. Two Way Mirror

I have only ever wanted you to see me.
All my life, I have been on the other end of a two way mirror.
I just wanted us to see each other.
But oh foolish me.
All my life, I have mistaken a two way mirror for a clear glass sheet.
I wanted you to see who I was.
Without filter.
Me.
With all my quirks and flaws.
How was I to know, that while I could see you that way,
you only ever saw yourself.
All my life, I have been so naive.
I have shared my secrets and woes to a seemingly transparent pane.
The two way mirror,
so beguiling in its design, played tricks upon my hopeful eyes.
Oh, how this mirror decieved me,
betrayed my yearning for reciprocity.
While I could see it all,
you could see what was all to you.
All my life, I have felt the bitter cocktail of frustration boil through my veins.

How was I to know, that you only saw yourself?

How was I to know, that mutual vision was a long lost dream?

How was I to know, that the clear glass sheet was nothing but

a two way mirror?

You could not see me, I learned after years.

Realisation quickly turned into rage.

How dare the two way mirror taunt me?

Offering a tantalizing glimpse of connection,

only to deny me authentic exchange.

All my life, the two way mirror left me stranded in a wasteland

of false perception.

I thought of breaking it,

reducing it to shards of shattered illusion.

Fortunately, I had too much pride.

Why should I break it?

All your life, you knew you could not see me.

All your life, you didn't even try.

All your life, you stood proud in front of your own reflection.

Sadly, sometimes,

regret,

my sullen companion,

tugs at the edges of my consciousness.

I learn to ignore it.

I paint the mirror opaque.

I realise that to me,

your presence is as real as any illusion.

27. Love Myself?

"Love yourself."
That's the thing, I always did.
So don't tell me to love myself during heartbreak.
I love the woman that I am, and because I do,
I allow her to feel pain and grief.
Those are only forms of love,
for another soul, or for mine.

28. Bloodless

Did you intrude? Without apology?

Without an ounce of shame or guilt?

They never said a word, leaning over the burgundy wood.

Absence of compassion enabled your treachery too.

By now, you'd think they would utter a word,

You found great pride in every inch of your skin.

You felt like a unbeatable weapon.

Like a hammer piercing nails into their fence.

And when they left, still without a word,

You felt like you had every right to point every finger of yours

at them.

29. Spring is Here

Spring is here.
As shoots spring from the soil,
a spring in my step appears.
I see the people around me,
and the edges of my lips can't help but spring up in glee.
Oh, how I've waited for spring.
How I've waited for spring all winter long.
For spring brings more warmth to my home than the summer
sun ever could.

30. The Ribbed Cage

The ribbed cage holds savage lions.
It contains vicious beasts, the wildest of all.
The same cage, carries my pulsing heart.
So don't mistake kindness for lack of strength.
Don't mistake warmth for lack of fortitude.
Don't mistake intimacy for weakness.
For why would one cage the powerless?

31. Happy Endings

So true to me as the ground I stand on, when it's new.

I was just a child, when I fell for the ruse once.

I was a fool to believe that every flame I encountered next was as magnificent.

I grieved and I grieved till I made peace with being lonely in remembrance of the ruse.

I lived with the remorse that it was only the first ruse, which wasn't.

That was until I saw a glimpse of the ruse again, shielded in the same heart.

A different form of the ruse, but equally, if not more strong.

And I thought of it, often, during the worst, best, and every little moment.

With an inch of regret, I still longed for the form I met first.

I refused to believe in a happy ending, having rarely witnessed one.

Steadily, I realised how lucky I was.

Not only to find that ruse again, but to find the ruse in you, both times.

And I now know why it had to be twice.

Because the first ruse made me feel everything, all at once, and I thought that was how it is to be.

It was the second ruse that made me realise that a ruse doesn't have to make me feel anything but only as real as the ground I stand on.

32. Alchemist's Elixir

Laminating its own creations,
the silver veil let loose.
Their eyes glimmered at the sight of opportunity,
as the wooden window frame softly rattled.
Nocturnal artist.
Pattered its palette on bamboo leaves.

33. Scars of Gold

You show them your scars,

They learn where you hurt the most.

The gold fills the gaps in your skin,

They wear the rags of the poor.

People say leeches aren't easy to rid off,

Why don't they speak of gold diggers?

I fence with all your swords but you lift up a knife.

I bring a loaded gun but your knife it still cuts.

You creep like a demon from a future life.

I saw your eyes glitter golden.

Your face always points to my scars of gold.

Oh sweet gluttony, don't you forget about me.

Don't forget about the gold in my veins.

I pray, stay here, begging to let go,

But my mind keeps glueing these broken strings.

You bury the knives you opened my scars with,

I forget that sharper are my wings.

I soar to the clouds till the seventh,

You drag me down after the eight.

I fence with all your swords but you lift up a knife.

I bring a loaded gun but your knife it still cuts.

You creep like a demon from a future life.

I saw your eyes glitter golden.

Your face always points to my scars of gold.
Oh sweet gluttony, won't you forget about me.
Don't let this bleeding go to vain.

34. A Few Words

I will only speak a few words,
And hope they bring change.
A thousand words can say the same thing,
But I hope the few of mine are of range.
I do not believe in speeches.
I hope my words only end in exchange.
The way a few words spread into phenomenon.
I know many find it strange.
So I will only speak a few words,
And hope they bring change.

35. The Unheard Song

I heard a song, knowing not what it was.

Grief's sorrowful melody taught me the peril of tying a song to a person.

For once the knot that tied us comes undone, so does the tune with every word.

But this song, I didn't know what it was.

The words, the beat, it was all unfamiliar.

How is it, that somehow, it still, reminded me of her?

And I never heard it again.

Because for the life of me, I couldn't find it.

Believe me, I searched.

Befitting, isn't it?

All I know is that in that moment, I only heard one song.

And that song was you.

36. Grey

The freshly poured cement I trudged through to reach you.

The clouds on the days you were around.

The armour I wore near you.

The metal dishes against the floor that your voice overpowered.

The walls I built to keep you afar.

The elephant in every room with us.

The ghosts that wander around the graves of those you abandoned.

The keys you used to lock me out.

The silver you tried to distract me with.

The bridges you made me break.

The nickels you took for yourself.

The smoke from my candle you blew out.

The only colour you don't steal from the lives of those around you.

The blades your words were as sharp as.

The bags under my eyes that grew tired of you.

37. One for the money, Two for the show, Three to make ready, And four to go

One for the money, Two for the show, Three to make ready, And four to go.
One for the puzzle, Two for the piece, Three to connect, And four to find peace.
One for the maze, Two for the guide, Three to navigate, And four to abide.
One for the footprints, Two for the trail, Three to forge a path, And four to unveil.
One for the needle, Two for the thread, Three to weave stories, And four to be read.
One for the money, Two for the show, Three to make ready, And four to go.

38. A Scared Man's Wisdom Tooth

Have you ever been a scared man's wisdom tooth?

A man woke up with gnawing pain in his gum.

It was only a wisdom tooth, finding its way out of the gum.

Indeed, the wisdom tooth was a burden to keep.

However, the man knew removing the tooth would hurt more.

So the wisdom stayed in the scared man's mouth.

Unwanted, yet needed to prevent the pain of its removal.

39. What is it?

In realms of riddles, deep and obscure,

Lies a word, enigmatic and pure.

With three letters it emerges, a cryptic design,

Yearning for discovery, its essence to define.

Yet when two more are woven in its spell,

The word retreats, a fading whisper it tells.

40. Shadows

You promised that you'd stay,

But you left me anyway.

You promised to ignore me,

But your shadow followed me.

Is a promise really so hard to keep?

I ran for the sun,

But your shadow grew sharper.

You left me undone, And time healed

But it rusted my armour.

Not a typical hit and run,

When your shadow sprints after me forever.

Your shadow buried in this soil,

I finished it with a tombstone.

Didn't know my tears of joy,

Could turn you to a ghost.

I'm tired of being held hostage.

I ran for the sun,

But your spirit grew darker.

You left me undone, And time healed

But it rusted my armour.

Not a typical hit and run,

When your ghost only goes hell for leather.

You finally kept a promise.

You left me with some piece.
But sometimes you take a dagger to it,
And haunt me in my sleep.

41. Don't Worry, it's Just a Sock

Seen stranded,

the poor thing was pitied by every passerby.

A sock separated from the other.

Lost.

The archetype of the prodigal wanderer.

It searched.

It longed for what was now popularly referred to as the 'missing sock'.

The sock ventured from corner to corner,

dodging dust bunnies and piles of forgotten clothes.

Daring enough, it slid into corridors of abandon.

A stoic protagonist in the theater of unpaired garments.

After much independent adventure, it longed for its other half.

Only a product of threads.

Yet it embodied human desire of companionship.

Forced to drag itself, with the weight of burden of unshared moments.

The sock mournfully cries.

It cries till it's soaked in its own tears of unrequited belonging.

The sock still searches today.

Every night, it still wishes to wake up next to the missing sock.

42. Thank You

Thank you.

Thank you for love.

Thank you for the love in mom's eyes that shine.

Thank you for the love that radiates from dad.

For this love, I'm forever grateful.

Thank you.

Thank you for wisdom.

Thank you for packing lessons in life's every twist and bend.

Thank you for turning the empty statement "everything happens for a reason" into a core belief.

Thank you.

Thank you for the pain.

Thank you for loss and thank you for failure.

Thank you for the heartbreak and tears.

For I would not understand the importance of happy moments in the absence of sadder ones.

Thank you.

Thank you for passion.

Thank you for making my eyes gleam when I talk about the little things I love.

Thank you for helping me understand the world by doing what I love.

Thank you.

Thank you for memories.

Thank you for the scrapbook that my mind is.

Thank you for letting me flip through the pages, and see how I have grown.

Thank you for letting me remember the people who I grew up with.

Thank you.

Thank you for change.

I know there is no growth without it.

Thank you for pushing me.

Thank you for what once seemed uncomfortable.

Thank you.

Thank you for people.

Thank you for giving me joy through the hearts of others.

Thank you for surrounding me with people who make every experience the best it can be.

Thank you.

Thank you for me.

Thank you for the person I am.

Thank you for the person I used to be.

Thank you for the person I will be.

I always want to give her love.

Thank you.

43. Forgery

Why form a bond, when there's always the risk of it breaking?
Distress, dismay, dread.
This is why I don't form, I forge.
I draw an elegant design of what commitment looks like to an
innocent eye.
I refuse to be a part of what may be real.
I have become a master of craft and con.
Many view it as a stance of power,
and on some days it might just be.
But truly, it is only a manifestation of foreboding.
I have learned to dabble with illusion,
where my every move is a ruse.

44. Handwritten Letters

• 51 •

When ink spilled on parchment,
like gold molten.
Handwritten letters,
a forgotten tradition.

45. Pot of Soup

I stirred the wooden ladle.

It didn't need much stirring,

It was just a pot of soup.

All things mixed, I stirred anyway.

It was just a pot of soup.

But if it was truly, just a pot of soup, then how come, it deciphered the aspects of joy?

Synergy: when the output of the whole system is greater than the output of its individual components.

How often I've read this.

But for once I saw it, in a pot of soup.

Close to a mimicry of life.

The soup's surface shimmered, just like the glow of little moments that make experiences grand.

So I stirred the wooden ladle.

It didn't need much stirring,

It was just a pot of soup.

All things mixed, I stirred anyway.

46. I Would Rather Not Know

My internal debate.

Does foreknowledge of farewells bring respite from sorrow's grip?

If you know,

you dread the day,

the moment it ends.

I figured the point was to make the most out of what is left.

Yet, knowing casts a pall,

a ticking bomb marring the sweet symphony.

Agony prevails until the tomb of the moment is reached.

On the other hand,

If you don't know,

you regret.

What if I missed the essence of final encounters?

What if this is the closing chapter?

What if-

That's when I learned the lesson of gratitude.

I learned to not fret.

Thanking constructs the staircase to rapture.

And to thank, uncertainty is key.

If each moment ends with gratitude for it,

there is only felicity to look back to.

My conclusion.

It's alright to not know when it ends.

47. The Ringmaster's Call

In the larger scheme of things,

parallel to a large circus if you will,

stands the one who controls it all.

The ringmaster.

When the need arrives,

for a decision maker, reliable and strong,

the ringmaster appears.

The sweet position of authority.

The acts, the costumes, the props,

the ringmaster oversees it all.

A ringmaster, you.

A ringmaster, me.

Ultimate power, over only our own acts.

Your acts, I could comment on, but never call and command.

48. Her

She remains nameless,
erased from conversation,
fatigued tongues reluctant to utter her name.
Her voice,
which was finally being heard after years of torment,
once again,
feels suffocated,
overpowered,
smothered in indifference's cold embrace.
Her voice,
a hymn of liberation,
has once again been reduced to a faint whisper.
She feels her cause being discarded,
that too,
with such ease.
She feels her presence being equated to a footnote,
in the pages of his story.

49. What Feeling Feels Like

Somehow, what brings in me the worst of fears and tears,
is what has shaped me to be who I am.
This is what feeling feels like.
The smallest of things to which my soul ties.
Given the go-by, by ordinary eyes.
This is what feeling feels like.
To detect a butterfly flapping its wings.
To hear a bell before it even rings.
This is what feeling feels like.
To sense the tremor of a fragile touch.
I grasp the weight of a moment's hush.
This is what feeling feels like.

50. Tarry

Rested on barren land,

All streams parched.

Me a marionette,

Fettered to monotony.

The tarrying night seemed to have taken root,

Cloaked me, in the drab veil of torpor.

Day's siren song resounds like a sonnet.

My body, still anchored to the sheets.

Ask me, not the night, how to tarry on.

This state, a mere forerunner to advancement.

Me a marionette,

Worn.

Lifted by the callous palm of responsibility.

Finally, you'd think.

You didn't expect what's next.

Me a marionette,

In a labyrinthine tangle of synaptic misfires.

A smokescreen of indistinctness.

Trapped.

A mere spectator.

An unmoored vessel, my mind chooses to be.

Is a hazy apparition, the best the world can be?

Me a marionette,

Dangling through the day.
Till the silk beckons.
Let night tarry again.

The End

The end of this book marks the start of our journey together. No matter the trials you face, the words on these pages will attest to your strength. When hardships arise, and your resolve falters, flip through these pages, let these words remind you of your might. This book is forever yours. Sing your song of sangfroid.

    - Diya Malhotra